A DINKUM AUSSIE DICTIONARY

Photography by Gary Lewis

Peter
Antill-Rose
& Associates Pty Ltd

63 Kingsway
Glen Waverley
Victoria 3150 Australia

Acknowledgements

First published in Australia in 1990 by:

Peter Antill-Rose and Associates Pty Ltd
63 Kingsway
Glen Waverley
Victoria 3150
Australia

Telephone (03) 562 0221
Facsimile (03) 562 0190

Photographs copyright© Gary Lewis 1990
Photographs by Gary Lewis
Pictorial editing by Allan Cornwell

Designed by Small Back Room Productions, Glen Waverley, Victoria
Typeset by Bandaid Productions, Fitzroy, Victoria
Printed by Griffin Press Limited, Marion Road, Netley, South Australia

ISBN 1 86282 089 9

Hassellblad and Ricoh camera equipment was used by the photographer in the production of this book

Ace. A man with a hunchback and a droopy shoulder (asymmetrical).

Actor. Pretending to be someone that you are not.

Aerial Pingpong. Australian Rules Football; a game whose rules are known only to Australians. Utterly confusing, it has four goal posts per end so that even near misses can be scored. The game can be identified by the strange flag-waving ritual of the people with white coats who are not, contrary to popular opinion, out of work doctors.

Alkie. Alcoholic, a down and out, a derro.

All dressed up and nowhere to go. Most often used when your girl-friend has stood you up.

Amber liquid. Beer.

Ankle biter. Young of the human species.

Ants in your pants. Fidgetty restless and nervous.

Apples. She'll be apples; everything will be O.K. She'll be right, she'll be sweet.

Arab. Insulting term for someone who has given you displeasure. 'You dirty rotten arab.'

Ardunno. I have no idea.

Argue the toss. To debate a point.

Arty-farty. Trendy, pseudo-artistic; can be said of yuppies, students, interior decorators and people's taste.

Arvo. Afternoon; 'See you the s'arvo.' 'Watcher doing Satday arvo?'. 'I won't be home til Sunday arvo.'

As useful as. This is a well known prefix to any group of words which points out someone's lack of help, contribution or assistance. Hence; as useful as a nun at a buck's night; as useful as a pork chop at a jewish barbecue.

Ashtray. 'Jeez mate, it was like kissing an ashtray.' His date was a heavy smoker.

Aunty. The A.B.C., or Australian Broadcasting Commission. (see axe).

Australian salute. Brushing away the flies from your face with your hand. Corks dangling from your hat were invented to reduce the numbers of salutes needed.

Axe. A favourite pastime of Aunty. She spends thousands of dollars developing programs and then when of course nobody watches them she axes them; she gets rid of them.

Axe handle. A standard unit of measurement. 'Jeez dya see that? She was at least two axe handles across the beam!'

Axehead. A short tempered employee likely to fly off the handle; not to be confused with a hammerhead who would swallow you in one piece.

B

Babe. An American WWII import; see Sheila.

Back. 'I've done me bleedin back in'; a familiar cry at work-care offices.

Back. That part of the anatomy which people are told to get off. These people tend to be nags, mother-in-laws, wives, girlfriends, rent collectors and generally people to whom you owe money.

Back Blocks. Constipation or more normally isolated country. To get the 'backblocks' in the 'backblocks' without a 'laxo' could mean eventual hospitalisation.

Back hander. A bribe or more commonly a popular arm movement directed at girlfriends, wives or children.

Back of beyond. See Black Stump.

Bad lot. 'They're a bad lot'; thieves, villains, crooks and more often than not your in-laws.

Bad news. Someone you don't wish to meet. They usually bring you a lot of bad luck.

Bag. Insult. 'She's an old bag'; always female, always unattractive. Beware at office parties of describing some sheila as an old bag to your boss; its probably his wife.

Bagging. To get or receive a bagging is to receive a lot of criticism.

The Baker. Known for having plenty of money (bread), but who's always in need of some extra dough, usually yours.

Bali belly. The runs, diarrhoea.

Ball tearer. Great, terrific. 'She's a real ball tearer'.

Bar. 'I won't have a bar of it'; to want nothing to do with it. Thought to have originated with the shearers' use of soap.

Barbie. The famous Australian pastime of turning indistinguishable cuts of meat into charcoal. The burnt offering is then liberally coated with a runny red substance full of artificial colourings and flavourings (see dead horse) and placed between two layers of thin white bread (not to be confused with cardboard). The whole thing is left to congeal with fat and a layer of blowflies. It is then eaten, washed down with copious quantities of beer.

Aerial Pingpong
goal umpire, V.F.L. football

Barbie.
a) name given to a worker at the local crematorium.
b) two chops short of a barbie; stupid.

Bark. Vomit.

Bark up the wrong tree. To get your facts all wrong.

Barney. An altercation usually non violent. 'We had a bit of a barney.'

Bastard. An extremely well used noun. Its correct application is an essential part of learning the Australian language. As a rule anyone or anything can be a bastard. Females are never bastards. Some examples of correct usage are listed below.
a) he's not a bad sort of bastard; — you like him.
b) that stupid bloody mongrel bastard; — you don't like him.
c) that poor bastard; you feel sorry for him.
d) he's a lazy bastard; he doesn't pull his weight.
e) he's a nasty bastard; you wouldn't trust him.
f) he's a clever bastard; he's smart.
g) he's a dozey bastard; he's not so smart.
h) he's a lousy bastard; he's a miser.
i) he's a weak bastard; he doesn't like to fight.
j) that bastard; you don't like him.

The list is endless; the world is your bastard so to speak.

Bastard. As an adjective it has a more restricted meaning; awful, horrible, definitely not enjoyable.
a) it was a bastard of a day.
b) it was a bastard of a meeting.
c) we had a bastard of a flight.
d) it was a real bastard.

Bastard of the Bush. The unsung folk hero of Australian dirty ditties. He is the original bastard.

Bastardise. To change from the original, especially language. Australia is probably the best in the world at this.
For example;
a) vegetables; veggies.
b) breakfast; brekkie.
c) biscuits; bikkies.
d) cardigan; cardie.
e) mosquitoes; mozzies.
f) Fremantle; Freo.
g) Rottnest Island; Rotto.
h) Christmas presents; Chrissie pressies.

A typical conversation might go 'I'm off to Freo after brekkie; I've wrapped me Chrissie pressies so the sarvo we can go across to Rotto. Will you bring me cardie and something for the mozzies. Oh and don't forget the bikkies and the veggies.'

Bash. A party, also
a) to ear bash; to talk incessantly.
b) I'll give it a bash; to try something.
c) bush bash; to attempt to walk from A to B in the mountainous regions of the country without using the path.

Bat. Ugly, usually directed toward mother-in-laws and wives, i.e. a fat bat, an ugly old bat.

Battler. Someone down on their luck, able to live by their wits with little income. 'Little Aussie Battlers' are underdogs who command respect because of their pride and willingness to battle on in tough times.

Batty. Crazy, often associated with senility. 'The poor old boy's gone a bit batty.'

Be. 'Owdya be!' An exclamation of wonder, astonishment or general disgust.

Beaut. Another example of the Australian bastardisation. Beaut by itself has become very toffee nosed middle class. 'Noosa is really beaut at this time of year.' 'You little beaut' is   more down market and describes such things as a small win at the races. 'You bloody beaut' would more aptly describe a winning ticket in Tatts or an author receiving a publisher's royalty payment.

Bed. 'He couldn't lie straight in bed.' A somewhat dishonest person.

Beer Gut. An expansion of the stomach. (usually irreversible). It comes from being influenced by too many TV commercials about thirst.

Bell. Front door, bicycle, church, birdcage. To be given a bell does not necessarily mean to be the recipient of one of the above. It can mean a call or a reminder. 'Give us a bell at three will you?'

Belly. To be lower than a snake's belly is to be a real bastard.

Bellyaching. Complaining.

Bellyfull. More than enough, far too much, (see gutfull) 'I've had a bellyfull of your bellyaching.'

Bellywhacker. Your first attempt at diving into a pool.

Better half. That person to whom one's pay packet is handed over — usually female.

Better than a jab in the eye with a sharp stick. Things have turned out better than one had first thought possible. You've just written your car off and someone gives you some new seat covers.

Bible basher. A religious nutcase, a jolly jehova, mormons etc. Immediately identifiable in the suburbs walking around in pairs. Grey suit for him, printed dress for her. They often walk with a limp from having their toes shut in the door.

Big. Prefix for various euphemisms.
a) big note; to boast.
b) big Smoke; the city.
c) big C; cancer.

Billabong. A dangerous waterhole for swagmen to hide in.

Billy. A dirty old pot in which only swaggies and campers make tea. The blacker the pot, the better the tea. It is synonymous with the bush. To put tea bags in a billy would be to invite thunderbolts from heaven.

Bit of a brothel. An ungodly mess.

Bite. To have the bite put on you is to have someone wanting to borrow money from you.

Bite your bum. To tell someone to do that is to tell them that you are not going to comply with their wishes.

Bitsa/bitser/bitzer. A mongrel dog.

Bitumen blonde. An aboriginal female.

Black Stump. The mythical landmark indicating the outer extremities of Australian civilization. To live 'Beyond the Black Stump,' is to live in a region where few people ever venture. To be the best or biggest turkey 'this side of the Black Stump' is to have no equal.

Blake. Joe Blake, rhyming slang; a snake; the shakes.

Blind Freddy. An elusive character from Australia's past. His spirit lives on; he is often called upon to point out someone's physical or mental insufficiency. 'Haven't you finished cooking tea yet? Blind Freddy could do a better job with one hand tied behind his back.'

Bludger. Originally a person who lived off the earnings of a prostitute, now it has wider connotations. A 'Dole Bludger' is someone who lives off the unemployment benefit.

Blue. Various meanings;
a) make a blue; make a blunder.
b) have a blue; to get involved in a fight.

Bluey.
a) a swaggies blanket.
b) cop a bluey — a summons.

Boat People. Not from Sydney's Northshore or the Hawkesbury River but an assortment of illegal Asian migrants, mainly Vietnamese, landing on Australia's northern coastline.

Bod. The female body.

Bodgie. An Australian tough of the fifties and sixties. He wore velvet jackets, bright shirts and tight pants, narrowed at the ankle. Definitely not someone your daughter should bring home unless she was a 'widgie'. Today's usage refers to shoddy workmanship. 'Dya see his Merc sports Bazza? Welded in the middle — a real bodgie job.'

Bondi Tram. Shoot through like a Bondi Tram; a speedy departure (trams were discontinued in 1961 in Sydney).

Bonzer. Great, fantastic, terrific. She's bonzer mate, she's all right.

Boofhead. Idiot, imbecile.

Black Stump
Foggdam sunset, Kakadu, Northern Territory

Boong. Offensive term for aborigine.

Boots'n all. Wholeheartedly.

Bot. A scrounger, someone who's always 'putting the bite' on you.

Bottom of the harbour. Home of Italians in concrete boots and the records of many tax-evasion schemes.

Bourke. A holiday resort for masochists in central N.S.W. on the edge of the desert. The Back of Bourke — the back of beyond.

Bowerbird. An Australian native bird which decorates its nest with useless glittering objects. Also it means a petty thief.

Break. Give us a break; lay off, let's not get into an argument.

Brick. Indicates permanence, dependability, solid, also dense or stupid.
a) he's a brick; dependable, a tower of strength.
b) he's built like a brick dunny; he's solid.
c) thick as a brick; somewhat dense.
d) London to a brick; betting odds, a certainty.

Bride's nightie. A level of great speed. 'He took off like a bride's nightie.'

Brown dog. Term applied to your mother-in-law's cooking. 'By Christ her roasts would kill a brown dog.'

Buckley's. You've got Buckley's. You've got no chance at all.

Bull. Absolute rubbish, waffle, talking nonsense.

Bull's roar. An arbitrary measure of distance by which someone fails to do something. 'He didn't get within a bull's roar of kicking that goal.'

Bundy. Rum. Made in Bundaberg. Young girls dilute it with coke.

Bung.
a) to go bung; bankruptcy.
b) bunging it on; acting above one's station, putting it on.

Bunny. The fall guy. The poor so & so who cops it when his mates have shot through and not paid the rent.

Bush. That nether region of Australia that is at the heart of its folklore. Just because 90% of Australians live in cities, hate the bush with its heat, dust and flies and only drive through it in air conditioned cars takes nothing away from its magic.

To go bush. To run away from civilisation.

Bushed. Contrary to popular belief it means to be lost. If you get bushed in the city ask a policeman, or a grey ghost. If you get bushed in the bush consult a survival manual.

Bushweek. 'What do you think this is, bushweek?' This would be asked of an ignorant cockie behaving in the city as if he was still in the bush.

But. However. Always used at the end of a sentence. 'You can't always be right, but.'

Cab. First cab off the rank; the first person to move, taking an opportunity before someone else does.

Cabbage Patch. Early nickname for the state of Victoria due to its size and crops.

Cactus.
a) in the cactus; in trouble.
b) it's cactus; it's of no further use.

Cadge. To beg, steal or borrow but done in a friendly way.

Camel. He's a real camel; he turns to water as soon as anyone confronts him.

Cancer stick. Cigarette.

Captain Cook. Rhyming slang; a look.

Cark. To die; 'Poor old budgie carked it.'

Carn. Strange cry to be heard at the football 'Carn a Blues.' Meaning come on.

Cheese. The female head of the family; the old cheese, the old chook.

Chew the fat. Talk things over.

Chiak. To give someone the cheek or to have a go (verbally) at someone. 'Oi stop chiaking me you bloody mongrel.'

China. Rhyming slang. China plate, mate. 'Hello me old china.'

Chink. Chinaman.

Chippie.
a) a carpenter.
b) a Fish and chip shop.

Chloe. 'As drunk as Chloe', is to be very drunk indeed. In Australia we associate this with Chloe the nude of Melbourne's Young and Jackson's Hotel. However, the expression can be found in English dictionaries as early as 1822, fifty years before the painting existed.

Chock-a-block. Absolutely full.

Choke a brown dog. See brown dog.

Chook. A chicken.
a) 'I hope your chooks turn to emus and kick your dunny door in;' to be annoyed with someone.

Chook raffle. If your local footy team is playing badly it is said they would be better off playing the chooks and raffling the players.

Choof. Polite expression for go away. 'Oh choof off you pommy bastard.'

Chuck.
a) vomit, (see yawn).
b) chuck us the screwdriver; pass it.
c) chuck a seven; to throw a fit, to die.

Chunder. Vomit. Its origin is unclear.
Popular belief has it that it originates
from sea-sickness on ships; a warning to
people on the lower decks. 'Watch out
under;' hence chunder.

Claggy on the waggy. Your dog's got a
dirty bum.

Clayton's. A substitute. Originates from
the marketing of Clayton's non-alcoholic
drink, i.e. the drink you have when
you're not having a drink.

Clock. A blow. 'I clocked him one.'

Clout. Similar to clock.
a) I gave him a clout round the lughole.
b) to clout down; being forced to stop
   doing something generally by the law.
   'The cops clouted down our backyard
   still.'

Clucky. Keen to have a baby is 'to get all
clucky.'

Coathanger. Sydney Harbour Bridge.

Cobber. One's best mate, an antiquated
but well known Australian expression
for your best friend.

Cocky.
a) a noisy white parrot.
b) a farmer. Traditionally cockies have
   been 'Little Aussie Battlers.' (see
   battler). You still see them struggling

Damper
Baking damper in a bush oven

but usually in and out of air conditioned Volvos and Mercedes.

c) cane cocky; sugar cane farmer.
d) cow cocky; dairy farmer, also fruit cocky; wheat cockies, spud cockies, etc.

Cocky's cage. Suffering a massive hangover you would have 'a mouth like the bottom of a cocky's cage.'

Cocky's joy. Golden syrup. In the days of early settlement a 2 lb. tin of syrup would have cost a quarter the price of jam and was hence used as a sweetener. The ultimate disaster was to find bull ants in your Cocky's joy.

Cockies' Corner. The area in Federal Parliament occupied by members of the National Country Party.

Come.
a) come across; to give sexual favours.
b) come good; to improve after not doing too well. A bank robber turned priest would be said to have come good.
c) come up smelling of roses; to extricate oneself from a difficult situation.

Commo. Anyone politically to the left of Genghis Khan.

Compo.
a) he's on compo; he's on workers compensation; a disability pension for injuries received at work.

Conk. Nose. 'He's got a conk like a jewish winetaster.'

Cooe. Supposedly a call, to hail someone.

a) to get within cooe; to get within hailing distance of someone.

Cop. To receive, to be in receipt of.
a) cop this lot; have a look at this.
b) cop a bluey; (see bluey).
c) cop it sweet; take it easy, to have a quiet day, to get an easy time of it.
d) cop a bundle; to receive more than your fair share of trouble.

Cossie. A swimming costume; now superseded by 'bathers.'

Cow. A measure of difficulty, indicates that things are crook; a fair cow, a cow of a job, a fair cow of a day, etc.

Crack.
a) couldn't crack it for a smile; can't see the humour in it.
b) crack a tinnie; open up a cold beer.

Cracker. Not to have one is to be destitute.

Crack hardy. Stoic endurance. To crack hardy and not drop your bundle was to endure living in a hostile bush environment without giving in to it.

Cradle snatcher. A person who goes out with someone a lot younger than themselves.

Cranky. Bad tempered, miserable.

Crash. To bed down. Normally associated with intoxication and being incapable of getting home, so you crash wherever you are.

Crawler. Someone who hopes to extract

favours by flattery and because of that they are
a) lower than a snake's belly.
b) they have scars on their belly.
c) see gravel rash.

Creamed. Annihilated. 'The Blues were getting creamed in the last quarter.'

Crook. Not feeling well, sick, no good, rotten, bad.
a) I feel really crook; I'm not feeling well.
b) crook in the guts; stomach upset.
c) the weather's crook; the weather's bad.
d) things are crook; things are not going as planned.
e) the bloody beer's crook; it's probably not as cold as it should be.
f) she went crook at me; she yelled and abused me.

Crooked. Bent, dishonest. He was as crooked as a dog's hind leg.

Crooked Mick of the Speewa. A legendary Australian bush character whose exploits and achievements are as mythical as Speewa the sheep station from which Mick hails.

Crust. The way in which you make money. 'What do you do for a crust mate?'

Cut. Your share of anything. Get in for your cut otherwise you'll be cut out and if you kick up a stink you'll be told to cut it out.

D

D. A detective.

Dag. All the muck and grime stuck in the wool around the back end of a sheep.
a) a real dag; a bit stupid.
b) a bit of a dag; a card, witty.

Daggy. Someone with a dishevelled appearance.

Damper. A kind of bread substitute. Plain flour, baking powder and water. It is cooked in the ashes of a camp fire. Not for the fainthearted or those with dentures.

Dead. A small word with many idiomatic uses.
a) he's a dead cert; he can't lose.
b) do that and you're a dead duck; you'll regret it.
c) dead as a door nail; unmistakably very dead.
d) dead heart; Central Australia.
e) dead marine; an empty beer bottle.

f) dead set; absolutely true, is that right?
g) dead loss; completely and utterly useless.
h) dead from the neck up; dense, stupid.
i) dead to the world; asleep, quite out of it.
j) dead head; a useless person.
k) dead horse; (rhyming slang) tomato sauce.

Derro. See alkie.

Didn't come down in the last shower. I wasn't born yesterday.

Digger. A familiar term of address, first used for the goldmines and then the soldiers of WWI and WWII.
a) the Little Digger; Prime Minister W.M. Hughes.
b) the Dirty Digger; Rupert Murdoch.

Dill. An amiable fool whose intentions are mainly good, but he's often not the full two bob, is a bit light up top and therefore not quite right in the head.

Ding dong. A confrontation, both verbal and more often than not physical.
a) a bit of a ding dong; a bit of a punchup.

Dingbat. Don't be a dingbat; don't be awkward, don't be a pain in the bum.

Dingo. A native dog still to be found in the bush. Once hunted, there is now an organization formed for their protection.
a) watch him, he's a bit of a dingo; he's a cunning so & so.

b) dingo's breath; bad breath.

Dinky di.
a) he's alright, he's dinki di; he's a true
   blue he's O.K.
b) it's alright, it's dinki di; it's the truth.

Dip.
a) dip the lid; take one's hat off to
   someone.
b) dip out; not to succeed, to miss out, or
   to refuse to join in.

Dirty.
a) they did the dirty on us; they cheated
   us.
b) don't do the dirty on me; don't let me
   down.

Do your dough. Lose all your money,
generally at the races.

Doan go crook at me. Don't yell or get
upset with me.

Dob. To inform on someone. This is
very un-Australian, maybe because of
their convict roots Australians have a
reluctance to pass on information about
others to the authorities. If you dob on
your mates you're some kind of a mongrel.

Dog.
a) an informer in convict times.
b) dog's dinner; something or someone
   who is untidy or messy.
c) the dog's are barking; a red hot racing
   tip.
d) a dog tied up; an unpaid bill.

The Coathanger
Sydney Harbour Bridge at night

e) you rotten dog; you pain in the neck.
f) turn dog; to betray someone, to back out of a commitment.
g) dog and goanna rules; no rules at all.
h) drover's dog; formerly a cattle dog, now a reference to a leading politician.

Dogger. Someone who in the past trapped dingos. A bounty hunter collecting payment for dingo scalps.

Done like a dinner. To be totally beaten especially in sport.

Dong. To aim a blow.

Drag.
a) men in women's clothing.
b) drag queen; a homosexual who wears women's clothing.
c) main drag; main road.

Drongo. A stupid person, an idiot. To be a dill is unavoidable. To be a drongo is inexcusable.

Drum.
a) not worth a drum; worthless.
b) drum up trade; looking for business.
c) never ran a drum; to come in last.
d) the drum; the good oil, the truth.

Dubbo. A country bumpkin; he doesn't necessarily come from the town of origin.

Duco. Paintwork; a spiritual aura exists around the duco of panel vans.

Dud. No good, something that doesn't work.

Duds. Clothing, generally male.

Duff.
a) duff up; knock someone about.
b) duff someone's poddys; to steal their cattle.
c) up the duff; pregnant.

Duffer. A silly duffer. Polite expression for a fool.

Dunny. An outside toilet, a bog.

Dyke. See dunny.

E

Each way.
a) to bet, win or place.

Eagle. The day the eagle screams; pay day.

Earbash. Chew someone's ear off, to talk the hind legs off a donkey. Politicians take degrees in earbashing.

Eat the horse and chase the jockey. Extreme pangs of hunger. You can be so hungry you would
a) eat the jocks off a cocky.
b) eat the whiskers off a strangled yabbie.

Eighteen.
a) a keg of beer.
b) a Sydney Harbour sailing skiff.
c) an Australian Rules Football team.

Elbow. To be given the elbow; your girlfriend's given you the big heave-ho, the big E.

Esky. An insulated drinks cooler; packed with ice it keeps your tinnies cool for hours even on hot days. Eskys (Eskies) are now searched at major sporting events. It is sometimes illegal to bring alcohol into the grounds. The kids now get rip roaring drunk by hiding the bacardi in their coca-cola.

Ethnic. An expression designed to irradicate the derogatory terms for migrants settling in Australia.

Face.
a) face like the back end of a bus; ugly.
b) face like a Newcastle docker; even worse than ugly.

Fair dinkum. True and honest. Dinkum Aussies, dinkum mates are fair dinkum; they are 100% Kosher and can be relied upon.

Fair. Please be reasonable, hence
a) fair go.
b) fair crack of the whip.
c) fair suck of the sav.
d) fair suck of the saucebottle.
All the above are asking only for some semblance of justice.

Fall off the back of a truck. Obtaining goods by illegal means.

Fat.
a) fat guts; an overweight person.
b) fatso; same as above.

Feed. The mongrel's not worth a feed. He's no use at all.

Feeding time at the zoo. A slight on the manners of people at a function where everything is usually for free.

Fice. Face. 'I brekka your fice'. A migrant expression for I'm going to push your head in.

Five finger discount. Shoplifting.

Flake. Sharkmeat, sometimes known as snapper, barramundi, gemfish etc., depending which chippie you go to.

Flash as a rat with a gold tooth. Overkill. Someone who's overdone his appearance. Someone who's overdressed and everyone knows it.

Flatout. Busy.

Flea pit. An old cinema where the back rows were always full.

Floater.
a) a delicacy of Adelaide; a meat pie floating in pea soup, garnished with tomato sauce.

Flog. To steal, can also mean to sell, much to people's confusion. If you come home and the wife has flogged a stereo, you've either now got one each or none at all.

Fluff.
a) he fluffed it; he made a mistake.

Form.
a) in reference to horses, if your horse has got form, its winning races.

Derro
Down and out in Melbourne

b) in reference to humans if he or she is in good form, they're usually witty and humorous.
c) true to form; as you expected.
d) if they have form; they've got a criminal record.

Four b' two. An extremely handy sized piece of framing timber, ideal for smashing sense into people and animals.

Freebie. Something you get for nothing.

Freezing. Any temperature below 25°C, unless of course you live in Hobart where 25°C is a heat wave.

Front.
a) more front than Myers; a lot of nerve.
b) to front a situation; to confront it.
c) to front up somewhere; to turn up, to arrive, to appear.

Full. Drunk.
a) full as a boot; drunk as a skunk, extremely inebriated.

G

The Gabba. Wolloongabba Cricket Ground, Brisbane.

Galah.
a) a noisy pink and grey parrott or cockatoo.
b) a fool, or simpleton.

Game.
a) he's as game as Ned Kelly; brave fearless.

Garbage.
a) a load of garbage; to talk a lot of rubbish.
b) garbage guts; a person who eats a lot. (see chunder)

Garbo/garbologist. A refuse collector.

Gazob. A stupid idiot.

Gazza'n Bazza. Australia's two most popular street heroes; Gary and Barry.

Geebung. A native born Australian.

The Ghan. The train which runs from Adelaide to Alice Springs. Named after the Afghan camel trains which initially ran the supplies between these two towns.

Gibber. A stone or a rock. Australia is well known for its gibber plains or stony deserts.

Ging. A child's catapult, also called a shanghai.

Glad eye. An enticing look.

Go.
a) 'D'you wanna go mate?' An invitation to engage in fisticuffs.
b) go bush; run away from civilization.
c) go troppo; go bonkers, become mentally disturbed.

Goanna. Rhyming slang, piano.

Godzone. Not heaven, but the next best thing to it; one's own country.

Goer.
a) it's a goer; any idea or project which looks like it will work.
b) she's a goer; ideas which you might have for her look like they might work also.

Goodonya. At first thought to be a suburb of Moscow it is however a typical Australian expression of approval or encouragement.

Goog. Egg.

Googy egg. A child's version of the same egg.

Goomie.
a) a homeless aborigine.
b) someone who tickles the turps, a derro, a metho-drinker.

Goyder Line. In 1865 the surveyor-general of S.A., G. W. Goyder mapped out a line of rainfall, north of which was unsuitable for growing wheat.

Gravelrash. The scars suffered by those lower than a snake's belly. (see crawler).

Greaser. A crawler.

Greenie.
a) a native inhabitant of rainforests and wilderness areas which are threatened by progress. Greenies can be seen buried up to their necks in the ground or manacled to earth-moving equipment.

Grog. Alcohol.
a) on the grog; on the piss, drinking heavily.
b) grog on; extended drinking session.

Groper.
a) someone from W.A., a sandgroper.

Grouse. Good.

Gum digger. A dentist.

Gummys.
a) an old sheep.
b) gum boots.

Gum tree.
a) up a gum tree; in strife, in difficulties.

Gush.
a) to talk effusively.

Guts.
a) hate someone's guts; to loathe them.
b) spill your guts; confess.
c) in the guts; two up, as bets placed.
d) rough as guts; somewhat common in speech or appearance.
e) have someone's guts for garters; to seek revenge.

Gutzer.
a) to come a gutzer; to come a cropper.

Guzzle. To drink thirstily and noisily.

Guzzle guts. One who does the above.

H

Had.
a) to be had; to be cheated.
b) have had it; to be fed up with.

Hair.
a) hair of the dog; an alcoholic drink taken to relieve a hangover; a heart starter.

Hairy goat. His horse ran like one; badly.

Half cut. Drunk.

Half inch. Rhyming slang; pinch, steal.

Hambone. A male striptease.

Hard
a) put the hard word on him; you want a favour, you want to borrow a few bob.

Have a go ya' mug. Don't just stand there do something.

Hay, Hell and Booligal. If you've ended up here amongst the heat and flies then you're way out past the Black Stump without a doubt.

Eighteen
Sydney Harbour eighteen foot skiff

Head.
a) run around like a chook with its head cut off; a state of panic or disarray.

Heart starter. See hair of the dog.

Heave. To throw up, to vomit.

Heifer.
a) a girl or young woman.
b) she's got thighs like a Meerigum heifer; they're large and hairy.
c) heifer paddock; a girl's school.

Hen. A woman.

Hen's night. A 'girls only' night out. Often her last night out before getting married.

Hen's teeth. To be as scarce as hen's teeth; rare.

Hoick. To clear the throat and spit.

Homing pigeons. He couldn't lead a flock of homing pigeons; useless, inept.

Hooley. A wild party.

Hoon. Formerly someone who lived off the earnings of a prostitute, but now a term used for a show off. 'He drives around in his hot F.J. with his sunnies and fancy shirts; he's a real hoon.'

Hoyts. All dressed up like the man outside Hoyts; overdressed.

Hughie. God, or the powers above that can make it rain in the outback. 'Send it down Hughie.' Not to be confused with his cousin, the god of the surf who controls the size of the waves. 'Whip 'em up Hughie.'

Hump.

a) to get over the hump; to break the back of it, to get through the worst part.
b) to have the hump; to be in a bad mood.
c) hump the bluey; carry a swag.

Humpy. Originally an aboriginal bark hut. Now any rough or temporary dwelling.

I

Ice-cold. A can of beer. Australian beer should be drunk so cold that your lips stick to the can or glass.

Ickle. Little, small.

Idea-monger. Someone with brains, an inventive person.

Iffy. Suspect. 'That looks a bit iffy.'

Include me out. Don't include me.

Inked. Drunk.

Iron.
a) iron yourself out; to get drunk.
b) iron maiden; a strong willed woman.
c) iron man; a physically strong man.
d) iron man contest; a contest of strength and endurance at a surf carnival.
e) talk the leg off an iron pot; very talkative.

J

Jack.
a) Jack the Lad; a wide boy, see bodgie.
b) Jack'n Jill, rhyming slang, the bill, a dill, the pill.

Jacko. A Kookaburra.

Jacksie. Buttocks.

Jake.
a) she'll be jake; everything will be O.K.

Jesus freak. A Bible basher.

Jewish stocktake. Destroying by fire or flood one's own business in order to claim the insurance money.

Jocks. Undies.

Joe.
a) a bare bellied joe; a ewe.
b) joes; rhyming slang, the woes, depression.
c) Joe Blow or Joe Bloggs; the average citizen.

d) Joe Blake; rhyming slang, a snake (also see Blake).

Joey.
a) to carry a joey; pregnant.
b) to slip a joey; a miscarriage.

Joker. Any stranger. 'Who's that bloody joker then?' 'He's probably just some bloody blow in.'

Julia Creek. 'the beer is weak in Julia Creek'; it's not somewhere to visit.

Jungle-juice. Home brew. A rough alcoholic drink. A sure way to get a case of the Joe Blakes.

K

Kangaroo.
a) Kangaroo court; an unauthorised mock court put together with disregard for legal procedure.
b) Kangaroo valley; Earl's Court, London, home of many expatriate Australians.
c) Kangaroos in the top paddock; mad, daft, batty.

Kark. To kark it; to die, expire, cease to work.

Keep the bastards honest. Former Leader of the Democrats' pledge to the two major parties.

Keep your end up. To pull one's weight.

Kick.
a) the bucket; to die.
b) in the kick; in the pocket.
c) nothing in the kick; no money or financial resources.
d) the cat; vent your feelings of frustration on someone else.

The Ghan

The Ghan approaching Alice Springs from Adelaide

e) he couldn't get a kick in a stampede; he's useless.
f) on; to carry on, usually drinking.
g) in for a pressie; a whip around, a collection.

Kiss.
a) like kissing your sister; an anti-climax.
b) of death; any project given this is doomed to failure.

Kiwi. A New Zealander.

Knuckle sandwich. A punch in the mouth.

Koori. An aborigine.

L

La. Toilet, also lala.

Lad. A rogue; (see Jack the Lad.)

Lady's Waist. A beer measure named after the shape of the glass. Great confusion exists for the poor visitor travelling through Australia. Trying to order a beer can be quite confusing. The following table sets out a guide. (We take no responsibility however for what might be served up to you.)

Size	Vic	N.S.W.	S.A.	QLD.	WA.
220ml	glass	seven/ pony lady's waist	butcher	—	glass
225ml	—	—	—	glass	—
285ml	Pot	Midi	schooner	Pot	Midi
425ml	—	schooner	kite	—	—
575ml	—	pint	—	—	pot

Note the lack of references to N.T. and Tas; that is because in N.T. they have a measure called a Darwin Stubby which is two litres and is generally served in a

large bucket. In Tasmania they drink
their own brew which some people say is
a good approximation of beer. It even
looks like beer. This table should act
as a useful guide but if you get into
difficulties just ask for a beer.

Lair.
a) a flash jack; often brash and vulgar.
b) lairy; flashy.
c) lair it up; behave in a flashy way.
d) lairise; to behave like a lair.

Lammie. A lamington. Standard
Australian cake. Won in raffles and used
in fund raising. Not strictly for human
consumption.

Land of the Long Weekend. Known
for its public holidays, flexitime and
rostered days off, Australia has adopted
this title with pride.

Larrikin. Formerly a wild young man, a
lout; more often now mischievious, high
spirited and with little regard for
authority.

Larry. Very happy. 'Happy as Larry.'

Lash.
a) a thrill.
b) lash out; spend money freely, strike,
   or become verbally aggressive.
c) have a lash at; try or attempt.

Laughing Jackass. Kookaburra.

Lav/Lavvy. Lavatory, dunny.

Lemonhead. A surfie with bleached hair.

Life wasn't meant to be easy. A phrase coined by a former right-wing politician. Although it supposedly comes from Shaw's 'Back to Methuselah' where the full statement is 'Life wasn't meant to be easy, my child, but take courage it can be beautiful', it is commonly agreed that it comes from the right wing political manifesto, 'Life wasn't meant to be easy, but we're all right jack.'

Lily.
a) an effeminate man.
b) like a lily on a dustbin; neglected.

Liquid amber. Beer.

Liquid lunch. Lots of liquid amber down the cake-hole.

Liquid laugh. Lots of liquid amber back up the cake-hole; vomit.

Lippie. Lipstick.

Logie. Australian T.V. award. Your mates can bestow logies on you for various achievements such as keeping your head in a bucket of dishwater for two minutes whilst holding a pickled onion between your teeth.

Lolly.
a) do your lolly; lose your head, temper, do your block.
b) lolly legs; tall ungainly with long, gangly legs.
c) lollywater; any non-alcoholic drink.

London. See brick.

Loo. A toilet, the dunny.

Looker. An attractive female.

Lounge lizard. An older expression for a man who frequented the lounge bars of hotels in order to pick up women.

Lower than a snake's belly. A creep.

Low wheel. A prostitute.

Lucky Country. Australia in the 1960's from Donald Horne's book of the same name. Death of a Lucky Country indicates his feelings for Australia today.

Lucky shop. The T.A.B., a government run betting shop.

Lucky legs. Thin spindly ones. 'She's got lucky legs.' 'Yeah lucky they don't break.' Also, 'She's got Wednesday legs.' 'Yeah Wednesday gonna break.'

Lump.
a) stupid or clumsy. 'You great big lump'.

Lunatic soup. A strong alcoholic drink.

Lurk. A real Lurk, a top lurk; money for jam, a well paid easy job, often its illegal or somewhat dubious, that's why its well paid. 'What do you do for a crust?' 'I'm a dog dentist in Dubbo.' 'Sounds like a bit of lurk to me.' 'Yeah a real top lurk, money for jam.'

M

Mad. Insane.
a) mad as a gumtree full of galahs.
b) mad as a cut snake.
c) mad as mother-in-law's cat.

Mad. Angry.
a) mad as a meat axe.
b) mad as a maggot.
c) mad as a turk.
d) mad as a turkish barber.

Madwoman. A woman whose behaviour causes things to be in disarray or to get into a dreadful mess; hence something looks like a madwoman's breakfast/tea/lunch/hairstyle etc.

Maggie. A magpie.

Makings.
a) 'He's got the makings of a fine cricketer.' He's going to be a good cricketer one day. It could also mean he's got hold of Dennis Lillee's smokes (see below).
b) to ask if someone's got the makings is to enquire as to whether someone has

the necessary tobacco and paper to
make a 'rollie' (a roll-your-own
cigarette)

Mallee bull. Strong and fit.
a) 'Gazza's strong as a mallee bull.'
'Yeah and he's got the brains of one
too.'

Mangy. Mean.
a) he's a mangy mongrel.

Mantrap. A seductive woman.

Marble Bar.
a) until it rains in Marble Bar; never.
Marble Bar is a town in Western
Australia, one of the hottest driest
places in Australia.
b) until it rains in Marble Arch; always.
Marble Arch is in London where it
pours down all the time.

Merchant. A person notorious for his
outstanding success in certain behaviour.
a) a panic merchant; a real worrier.
b) a standover merchant; a bully boy.

Merry. Intoxicated.

Mick. A Roman Catholic.

Midge. A small person.

Migrant. Now a somewhat derogatory
term for someone recently arrived in
Australia. It has been superseded by
'New Australian.'

Milk bar cowboy. A tough bikie type
who frequents milk bars, not pubs;
usually gutless wonders.

Mind. A measure of normalcy. One can be drunk or freaked out of one's mind.

Mixed company. A gathering of people where ladies are present and language must be toned down.

Moggy. Someone's dearly loved pet usually to be found lying squashed by the side of the road.

Moll. A girlfriend or mistress.
a) surfie's moll; girlfriend of a surfie.
b) bikie's moll; girlfriend of a bikie.
c) politician's moll; his secretary.

Mondayitis. How the hard working average Australian feels about going to work any day of the week.

Mongrel.
a) a term of contempt.
b) a difficult task; a mongrel of a job, day etc.

Monthly. A menstrual period.

Mother's ruin. Gin, also grandad's downfall, aunty's ailment, dad's demise.

Mouth.
a) down in the mouth; unhappy, depressed.
b) shut your mouth; an order to keep quiet.
c) shut uppa your mouth; an order by 'New Australians' to keep quiet.

Mozzie. A flying disease carrier. They bite other disease carriers and then sink their dirty little proboscuses into the likes of you and I. In this way we are all at risk of catching malaria, ensephylitis, and maybe even AIDS.

Mug. A fool.

Mug lair. A flashily dressed young man with loud tastes and vulgar habits.

Mulga.
a) the bush.
b) go up the mulga; to venture out into the bush.

Mullet.
a) stunned mullet; an expression of utter disbelief.

Mullygrubber. A bowl in cricket in which the ball is delivered to the batsman along the ground. An Australian special in one day international matches.

Murrumbidgee.
a) a river in southern N.S.W.
b) Murrumbidgee jam; a spread made from brown sugar and cold tea, it makes your teeth fall out.
c) Murrumbidgee oyster; a drink made from raw eggs.

Mutt. A friendly canine of indeterminate parentage.

Mutton.
a) dead as a mutton chop; undeniably dead.
b) mutton head; stupid.

My oath. Certainly.

Myxo. A highly infectious viral disease in rabbits. Most Australian shooters are only capable of hitting rabbits with myxo which are half paralysed, but would adamantly deny it.

Narky. Bad tempered.

Naughty bits.
a) the good bits which they cut out of films before showing them on T.V.

Necessary.
a) 'Have you brought the necessary?' Have you brought the money.

Ned Kelly.
a) a reference to an unprincipled businessman.
b) as game as Ned Kelly; brave, fearless.
c) Ned Kelly's necktie; a hangman's rope.

Nelly's Death. Cheap red wine.

Nerd. A fool, an idiot.

Never Never.
a) imaginary desert country way out beyond the black stump.
b) to purchase goods on the hire-purchase/credit system.

New Australian. See migrant.

New chum.
a) originally a recently arrived convict, more lately a term for a British migrant.
b) inexperienced at something.

Niff. An unpleasant smell.

Night cart. A sanitary truck.

Noah's Ark. (Rhyming slang), shark.

Noastie. Air hostess.

Nobbler. A small glass of spirits.

No worries. A unique Australian expression of supreme confidence, uttered at times of extreme stress. It's 42°C in the shade at the M.C.G., the beer's just run out and you're dying of thirst. Your friend Gazza says 'No worries mate, she'll be right.' He smacks the guy standing next to him over the head with a handy chair leg and borrows the two dozen cold tinnies in his esky.

No-hoper. Someone with little intellect, money, or hope for the future.

Nose rag. A handkerchief.

No show. Not a chance, not even in the race, no hope of success.

Not on. 'It's just not on sport.' It just cannot be allowed.

Nuddy. Nude.

Nudge.
a) give it a nudge; try something, to make an attempt.

Land of the Longweekend
Surf beach, Coolangatta, Queensland

attempt to become legless through excessive consumption of alcohol.

Nugget. A short muscular man.

Nuke. A nuclear device. Many councils in Australia have declared their cities nuclear free zones. In the event of war nuclear warheads will bypass these zones and land elsewhere. Australia does have its own 'Newk' but it only sells bananas and lends money except of course in those Newk clear free zones.

Number ones. An idiotic expression used by adults when their children ask to go to the toilet. It is obviously offensive to talk to your children about perfectly natural day to day bodily functions, and so we have devised this idiotic code. Number ones — wees. Number twos — poos.

O

Obscenity. Something which absolutely offends your moral senses. Fat, obese, beer bellied, beer swilling males are not obscene, merely ockers.

Ocker.
a) typical uncultured Australian, uncouth boorish and chauvanistic.
b) a real ocker; distinctively Australian good humoured and helpful.

Note; There is no difference between a) & b) above its the same man; a) is how others perceive the Australian male and b) is how he perceives himself.

Ockerina. The ocker's female counterpart.

Off. An extremely versatile word in the Australian language. For example at a badly arranged barbecue;
a) the beer's off; the keg tap's busted.
b) the meat's off; the blowies have got at it.

Oil.
a) dinkum or good oil; correct

information.
b) well oiled; drunk.
c) your car runs on the smell of an oily
   rag; it doesn't use much petrol.

Oldies/olds. Parents, or anyone over twenty as viewed by anyone under sixteen.

On.
a) on the bottle/turps; drinking
   alcohol to excess.
b) on the wagon; not imbibing alcohol.
c) on for young and old; a free for all,
   lack of restraint.

One-dayer. A game of cricket (see Mullygrubber).

Optic.
a) to have an optic at; to take a look at.

Orange-time. A half-time break in football, rugby etc. when each side would like to molest the other team's cheer squad, but they don't have the energy so all they do is suck on bits of citrus fruit.

Outback. That part of Australia in which 95% of Australians choose not to live. It is instead inhabited by 95% of Japanese tourists.

Outer.
a) On the outer; excluded from a group
   and probably sent to drink with the
   flies.

Owsyerottenbleedinluckeh?
Thought to be the longest word in the
Australian language it translates as
things are not turning out as planned, for
example when you blow the
housekeeping money at the races.

P

Pacifier. A policeman's truncheon.

Pack.
a) death; afraid.

Parson's pushbike.
a) he shot through on the parson's pushbike; whereabouts unknown.

Palooka. Don't be such a palooka. Don't be so clumsy and stupid.

Paralytic. Very drunk.

Pash. Passion.

Pash-on. A prolonged heavy kissing, petting, groping session.

Perk. Throw up.

Pig's bum/ear. Exclamation of denial or annoyance etc. Often shortened to 'Pigs' in mixed company.

Piker. Someone who lets you down at the last moment.

Pineapple. To get the rough end of the pineapple; the worst end of a deal.

Pixies. Away with the pixies; off the planet, either drunk or insane.

Plastered. Drunk.

Plate face. An Asian migrant.

Pline. New Australian for jumbo-jet.

Plonk. Cheap, rough wine.

Plonk merchant/artist. Someone addicted to cheap rough wine.

Pod. In pod; pregnant.

Point Percy at the porcelain. Urinate.

Pom/Pommy. A person of English ancestry, origin unknown. Some thoughts are;
a) POME: Prisoner of Mother England (possible).
b) POME: Person of Much Education (their version).
c) POME: from Pomegranate, bright red skin like a pom in the sun (popular).

Pommy bastard. A person of English origin, the term can be offensive or not depending on context. For example;
a) he's not a bad sort of Pommy bastard, you like him.
b) he's a stupid, mongrel Pommy bastard; you don't like him.

Outback
Uluru (Ayers Rock), Northern Territory

Ponce.
a) pimp.
b) ponce about; to behave in a foolish way.

Poophead. A general insult.

Poppy show. Girls indecently showing off their thighs and underwear. In today's age of micro-bikinis, G-strings and topless bathing one marvels at the outraged morality of showing off thighs and underwear!

P.O.Q. To depart hurriedly.

Possum.
a) play possum; feign illness etc.
b) stir the possum; create a disturbance.
c) hello possums; a traditional Australian greeting.

Potboiler. A person who writes inferior pieces of literature purely for monetary gain. (With the sort of royalties publishers pay these people are all bankrupt today.)

Prawn. A bit of a fool.
a) don't come the raw prawn; don't try to deceive.
b) prawnhead; a term of abuse.

Pro. A prostitute. Australia is so progressive it even has resident pros at golf and tennis clubs.

Pud.
a) pulling the pud (metaphorically), it implies timewasting. 'Come on

sunshine, don't stand there pulling
your pud.'

Puke.
a) to vomit.
b) a very sick nuclear warhead.

Pull.
a) your finger out; get a move on.
b) a fast one; to deceive.
c) someone's leg; to joke.
d) a swiftie; to deceive.

Push. (archaic usage) a street gang. i.e.
a) the push from Wooloomooloo.

Quid. Not the full quid; brain damaged or retarded.

Rack off. To leave, to go, an order to go.
a) rack off hairy legs; please leave.
b) he racked off ages ago; he left hours ago.

Raining. An expression of bad luck, e.g.
a) if it was raining mansions, I'd be hit by a dunny door.
b) if it was raining champagne, I'd be hit on the head by a broken glass etc.

Raise. He was so drunk that he couldn't even raise a smile; a reference to alcoholic impotence.

Rapt. Enthusiastic.

Rare. Expressions change depending upon the rarity of what is being bought, sought after or commented upon.
a) as rare as a Jewish charity donation.
b) as rare as a list of Italian war heroes.
c) as rare as hen's teeth.
d) as rare as an Irish book of wisdom.

Rat.
a) a despicable person.

b) to rat on; turn on your friends.
c) like a rat up a drainpipe; very quickly.
d) smell a rat; to be suspicious.
e) ratbag; unsociable, not likeable.

Rattler.
a) red rattler; Melbourne's old red trains.
b) jump a rattler; to board a train illegally, to avoid paying a fare.

Razoo. He doesn't have a brass razoo; he's destitute, penniless.

Real.
a) for real; absolutely, definitely.
b) get real; similar to don't come the raw prawn, but less expressive.
c) real drop kick; a nerd, a right fool.

Red.
a) red hots; (rhyming slang) the trots, horse racing.
b) red ned; cheap red wine.
c) red light district, formerly a street with many brothels, now a street with many doctor's surgeries.

Reffo. A refugee, especially from the period before WWII, from Europe.

Reginalds. (Rhyming slang) Underwear; from Reg Grundy's — undies.

Richard.
a) to have had the Richard; to be ruined, to be worn out, polite form of had the dick.

Ridgie-didge. On the level, O.K.

Rip.
a) let rip; utter profanities.
b) rip off; to swindle.
c) rip off merchant; a swindler.
d) you little ripper; an expression of joy.
e) a ripping good yarn; a good story,
     nearly always exaggerated.
f) ripped; stoned or drunk.

Robber's dog. Off like a robber's dog; a measure of haste.

Roitnow. Immediately.

Rollie. See makings.

Rooster. A rooster one day, a feather duster the next; the uncertainty of a run of luck, penned from a comment about being a politician.

Rough. Severe, hard, unpleasant, vulgar, etc.
a) rough edge of the pickle; a raw deal.
b) rough as guts; the wine's unpleasant.
c) rough as a pig's breakfast; extremely vulgar.
d) rough as a skinhead's crotch; as above.
e) cut up rough; behave violently, upset.
f) roughing it in Toorak; living it up.

Rug rat. See ankle biter.

Rubbedy dub. (Rhyming slang) Pub.

Rumble bum. Someone prone to passing wind.

One-Dayer
Day/night match, World Series cricket, Melbourne Cricket Ground

Salute.
a) Australian salute; to brush the flies away from your face.
b) Barcoo salute; as above.
c) Afghan salute; to brush the flies away from your bum.
d) salute the judge; a jockey crossing the finishing line.

Sandgroper.
a) a resident of Western Australia.

Sanger. A sandwich.

Sanny cart. Sanitary truck.

Sanny man. Its driver.

Sauce. See suck.

Sav. See suck.

Sausage.
a) sausage sizzler; a BBQ to raise funds for the local school, not some strange form of hideous torture.

Scorcher. A hot day. Real scorchers are bastards.

See a man about a dog. To go to the toilet.

Set.
a) dead set; true, certain.
b) set up; what's the set up? How are things organized?

Shake.
a) hands with the wife's best friend; urinate.
b) the shakes; the D.T.'s.
c) in two shakes; very shortly.

Shark bait. Someone who swims in a spot well known for shark attacks. Windsurfers always sail near surfers because surfers make better shark bait.

She'll be right/apples/jake. Optimistically everything will be O.K.

Sheila. A girl or female. The other half of Australia's well known duo Bruce and Sheila.

Shicker. To get on the shicker, to intend to get drunk, hence shickered, he succeeded.

Shypoo. Cheap and nasty plonk.

Sickie. A day taken off work with pay because of illness, but more likely to go to the beach or the tennis i.e. too crook to take a sickie. You don't want to waste a sick day by being at home in bed ill, you might just as well go to work.

Silent Policeman. A small raised device placed in the road to guide traffic mainly in N.S.W. They are designed actually to knock over motorbike riders and to rip sumps and exhaust pipes off cars.

Skirt. A woman or girl.

Skite.
a) to boast or brag.
b) what New Australians do on ice.

Skun. To drink all someone's booze.

Slip slop slap.
a) a warning to put on suntan cream.

Smoko. Ritual tea-break time.

Snag. Sausage.

Snake's belly. See lower than.

Snaky. Irritable.

Sneaker. A shoe with soft rubber soles that make no noise when creeping around female dormitories.

Snowbunny/ski bunny. A young woman who frequents a ski resort, more for the apres-ski than the skiing itself. Older males should be careful when chasing snow bunnies due to the effect of the high altitude on the respiratory system.

Soapie. Serialised T.V. dramas.

Sook. A wimp.

Sool. To incite to violence.

Sort. A good sort.
a) an attractive female.

b) a reliable bloke.

Spag. An Italian.

Spag bog. Spaghetti Bolognese.

Sparrowfart. Dawn, early morning. He was up at sparrowfart.

Specimen. A New Australian astronaut.

Speedos. Bathers, cossie.
a) he's got his speedos on arse about; he's slow.

Speewa. The home of Crooked Mick, Blind Freddie's cousin.

Spit.
a) spit chips; extremely annoyed.
b) the dummy; lose one's temper.
b) the big spit; to vomit.

Spew. To vomit.

Spewin'. A measure of how you feel about things. You can miss the train and be spewin — put out. You can miss out on one number in Tatts and be really spewin.

Stack on a blue. Quarrel. Start a fight.

State. Australia shows its bad taste by describing the various states on the car licence plates. State of Excitement; W.A. The Garden State; Victoria. The Festival State; S.A. The Premier State; N.S.W. The Holiday Isle; Tasmania. The Outback Territory; N.T. (it's not a state). The Sunshine State; QLD. The Nation's

Capital; A.C.T. At the time of going to press the new plates had been issued we believe. State of Exhaustion; W.A. The Pesticide State; Victoria. In No Fit State; S.A. State of Intoxication; N.S.W. We're now on the Map State; Tasmania. We'd like to be a State; N.T. The Police State; QLD. The Country's in a State; A.C.T.

Stir.
a) the possum; see possum.
b) crazy; crazy as a result of being in jail for so long.

Stitch up a wood duck. To fool a gullible person.

Stone motherless; flat stony broke.

Stoush. A punch up, a brawl.

Strewth. A Clayton's oath, from God's truth.

Strides. Trousers.

Strife. Trouble.
a) in more strife than Flash Gordon.
b) in more strife than a one armed poster hanger in a gale.
c) in more strife than a possum in a thunderbox.

Straight. Heterosexual.
a) straight up; for real.

Strain.
a) the potatoes; urinate.

Stubbies. Shorts, an Australian uniform, tight fitting round the crutch to prevent the beer gut from falling any lower. Worn to all major sporting and social events such as the cricket and BBQ's.

Stunned. See mullet.

Suck.
a) fair suck of the sav/sauce bottle; fair go mate, be reasonable.
b) sucked in; fooled.

Sun. The sun shines out of his bum; he has a somewhat high opinion of himself.

Sundyarvo. Sunday afternoon.

Sunnies. Sunglasses.

Surfers. Surfers Paradise. A popular Queensland Tourist resort where the sun sets behind the high rise buildings, leaving the beach in total darkness by two in the afternoon.

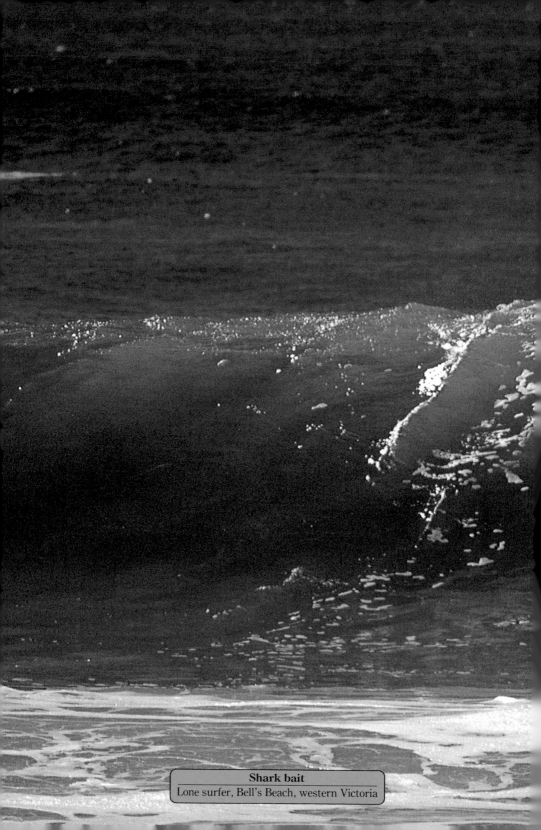

Shark bait
Lone surfer, Bell's Beach, western Victoria

T

Talent. 'There's not much talent here tonight, they're all molls and paper bag jobs.' The girls at the dance are not exactly Miss World entrants.

Talk.
a) the hind legs off a donkey; at great length.
b) a leg off an old iron pot; as above.

Tallarook. Things are crook in Tallarook; everything's not as it should be.

Tanked up. Intoxicated.

Tar brush. A touch of the tarbrush; some negroid/coloured features in a person's appearance.

Technicolour yawn. Vomit.

Ten past one and not a bone in the truck. You haven't achieved a thing.

Ten pound pom. Not an indication of his weight but how much it cost him to emigrate.

Territory confetti. Ring pulls from beer cans.

Thick. Dense, dimwitted, hence
a) thick as a brick.
b) thick as two short planks.
c) thick as a wharfie's waistline.

Three axe handles. Width of your mother-in-law's bum.

Three snags short of a barbie. A mental lightweight.

Throne. The toilet.

Throw.
a) up; vomit.
b) a seven; your time's run out, became unconscious, become very angry.

Thunderbox. An old time outside toilet with no plumbing, a builder's toilet.

Tied up. A dog tied up; an unpaid bar tab making you reluctant to return.

Tinny.
a) a beer.
b) lucky.

Tired and emotional. Euphemism for blind drunk, especially used in print when talking about politicians and heads of state, etc.

Toe.
a) hit the toe; off in a hurry, to escape.
b) toe-jam; dirt which collects between the toes.
c) toe rag; a down and out.

Tooth fairy. An improbability. 'Who do you think did it, the bloody tooth fairy?'

Top sort. An attractive young female.

Troppo. Mental illness from living for too long in the tropics.

Trots.
a) harness racing.
b) to have the trots; diahorrea.

Turkey. A no hoper; a wimp.

Turps. On the turps; drinking to excess.

Two.
a) bob lair; flashily dressed in cheap clothes.
b) pot screamer; a cheap drunk.
c) shakes; I'll be back in two shakes i.e.

Two wheeler. (Rhyming slang). Sheila.

U

U-ey. Chuck a u-ey; to make a U-turn. This is the classic Australian manoeuvre of turning your car around whilst causing the maximum chaos to other road users.

Ump. 'E's got the 'ump'; irritable.

Underdaks/duds. Undies, underwear.

Under the weather. Crook in the guts, often from an over indulgence of alcohol.

Unwashed. The great unwashed; Pommy migrants.

Ute. The home of a workman's dog, Blue heelers, German Shepherds, Dobermans, Rottweilers, Bull Terriers etc.

Vegemite.
a) a black gelatinous mass of vegetable extract and salt, spread on bread. Australians abroad have been known to suffer withdrawal symptons from lack of vegemite.
b) a happy little vegemite; a happy little child.

Verbal diarrhoea. To talk, usually nonsense, at great length.

Vino. Cheap red wine.

W

Wacker. A fruit cake, mad as march hare.

Wanda. Seldom used, aboriginal expression for whiteman.

Weaker sex. Female (except for female mud wrestlers.)

Wet.
a) wet enough to drown a duck; very wet.
b) wet the baby's head; celebrating the baby's birth by getting absolutely drunk, a traditional Australian initiation ceremony.
c) wet bum and no fish; fruitless.

Whadaarya. A reply uttered in disbelief at the stupidity or naivety of the initial statement.

Wham, bam, thank you mam.
Anything done quickly, without fuss and unemotionally.

Thunderbox
A country dunny, South Australia

Whingeing Pom.
a) An insulting term for English migrants who dare to criticize this wonderful country and its warm-hearted, outgoing, carefree, generous law-abiding people (Australian version).
b) someone who misses soggy fish and chips, warm beer, black pudding and Margaret Thatcher (alternate version).

Whip.
a) fair crack of the whip; give us a fair chance, see also fair suck of the sav.

White ant. To undermine someone or their chances. It derives from the damage done by Australian termites.

Y

Yahoo. An uncouth yobbo.

Yawn. Mainly in technicolour; vomit.

Yob. A loutish oaf.

You're not wrong. Australian for you are correct.

Youse. Plural of you, as in you two. A smart piece of Australian linguistics not yet adopted by newsreaders.

You wouldn't be dead for quids. Something has occurred that you are glad you saw or experienced.

Zit. A pimple, acne.

Zonked. Comatose through drink.